D0118670

# Safety at Home

# Seguridad en la casa

## Dana Meachen Rau

Marshall Cavendish
Benchmark
New York

Your home is a fun place to play.

Be safe in your home.

———————❖———————

Tu casa es un lugar divertido para jugar.

Mantente seguro en tu casa.

Always pick up after playing.

You can trip on toys on the floor.

———————❖———————

Recoge siempre después de jugar.

Puedes tropezarte con los juguetes que están en el suelo.

Some toys can make babies *choke*.

Be sure to put away all the small pieces.

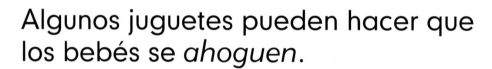

Algunos juguetes pueden hacer que los bebés se *ahoguen*.

Asegúrate de guardar todas las piezas pequeñas.

Do not run on the stairs in socks.

You could slip and fall.

---❖---

No corras por las escaleras
en calcetines.

Podrías resbalarte y caer.

Do not touch an *outlet*.

An outlet can give you a shock.

———◆———

No toques los *tomacorrientes*.

Un tomacorriente puede darte una descarga.

Check your bath before you get in.

Hot water can burn you.

Prueba el baño antes de meterte.

El agua caliente puede quemarte.

Only grown-ups should touch *medicine*.

Some medicines can make you
very sick.

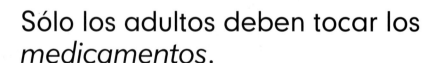

Sólo los adultos deben tocar los
*medicamentos*.

Algunos medicamentos pueden
enfermarte mucho.

Many cleaners can make you sick, too.

Do not touch them!

———————❖———————

Muchos limpiadores también pueden enfermarte.

¡No los toques!

Always cook with a grown-up.

Stoves can be very hot.

————◆————

Cocina siempre con un adulto.

Las estufas pueden estar muy calientes.

Put food back in the refrigerator.

Some foods can spoil and make you sick.

Vuelve a guardar la comida en el refrigerador.

Algunos alimentos pueden echarse a perder y enfermarte.

Be safe when you play outside, too.

Do not climb too high.

———————❖———————

Mantente seguro también cuando juegas afuera.

No trepes demasiado alto.

Play in your own yard.

Never talk to strangers.

———————❖———————

Juega en tu propio patio.

Nunca hables con desconocidos.

Be a safe kid at home.

———————❖———————

Sé un niño seguro en casa.

# Be Safe
## Estar seguro

**bath**
**baño**

**cleaners**
**limpiadores**

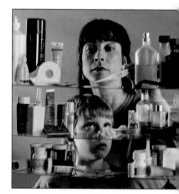

**medicine**
**medicamentos**

**outlet**
**tomacorrientes**

**stairs**
**escaleras**

**toys**
**juguetes**

**yard**
**patio**

## Challenge Words

**choke** To not be able to breathe or swallow.

**medicine** A drink or pill that helps you get better when you are sick.

**outlet** The holes in the wall for plugs.

**spoil** To turn rotten and unsafe to eat.

## Palabras avanzadas

**ahogar** No poder respirar ni tragar.

**echarse a perder** Pudrirse y volverse peligroso para comer.

**medicamento** Bebida o píldora que te ayuda a estar mejor cuando estás enfermo.

**tomacorrientes** Los agujeros para los enchufes que hay en la pared.

# Index

# Índice

## About the Author
Dana Meachen Rau is the author of many other titles in the Bookworms series, as well as other nonfiction and early reader books. She lives in Burlington, Connecticut, with her husband and two children.

## Sobre la autora
Dana Meachen Rau es la autora de muchos libros de la serie Bookworms y de otros libros de no ficción y de lectura para principiantes. Vive en Burlington, Connecticut, con su esposo y sus dos hijos.

With thanks to the Reading Consultants:
Nanci Vargus, Ed.D., is an Assistant Professor of Elementary Education at the University of Indianapolis.

Beth Walker Gambro is an Adjunct Professor at the University of Saint Francis in Joliet, Illinois.

Agradecemos a las asesoras de lectura:
Nanci Vargus, doctora en Educación, es profesora auxiliar de Educación Primaria en la Universidad de Indianápolis.

Beth Walker Gambro es profesora adjunta en la Universidad de Saint Francis en Joliet, Illinois.

Marshall Cavendish Benchmark
99 White Plains Road
Tarrytown, New York 10591
www.marshallcavendish.us

Library of Congress Cataloging-in-Publication Data

Rau, Dana Meachen, 1971–
[Safety at home. Spanish & English]
Safety at home = Seguridad en la casa / Dana Meachen Rau.
p. cm. — (Bookworms. Safe kids = Niños seguros)
Includes bibliographical references and index.
Parallel text in English and Spanish; translated from the English.
ISBN 978-0-7614-4780-1 (bilingual ed.) — ISBN 978-0-7614-4089-5 (English ed.)
1. Home accidents—Prevention—Juvenile literature. I. Title. II. Title: Seguridad en la casa.
TX150.R3918 2009
363.13'6—dc22
2009017260

Editor: Christina Gardeski
Publisher: Michelle Bisson
Designer: Virginia Pope
Art Director: Anahid Hamparian

Spanish Translation and Text Composition by Victory Productions, Inc.
www.victoryprd.com

Photo Research by Anne Burns Images

Cover Photo by *Getty Images*/Dave & Les Jacobs

The photographs in this book are used with permission and through the courtesy of:
*Getty Images*: pp. 1, 11, 28BL Jeffrey Coolidge; pp. 9, 28BR Margo Silver;
pp. 15, 28TR David Buffington; pp. 25, 29R Bambu Productions. *Corbis*: p. 3 Steve Cole;
p. 19 Jose L. Pelaez; p. 23 John-Francis Bourke/zefa; p. 27 Tracy Kahn.
*Alamy Images*: p. 5 David R. Frazier Photolibrary; pp. 7, 29L sciencephotos;
pp. 13, 28TL Jack Sullivan; pp. 17, 28TC Chris Pancewicz. *Photo Edit, Inc.*: p. 21 Myrleen Pearson.

Printed in Malaysia
1  3  5  6  4  2